Author:
Fiona Macdonald studied history at Cambridge University and at the University of East Anglia. She has taught in schools, adult education, and college and is the author of numerous books for children on historical topics.

Artist:
David Antram was born in Brighton, England, in 1958. He studied at Eastbourne College of Art and then worked in advertising for fifteen years before becoming a full-time artist. He has illustrated many children's nonfiction books.

Series Creator:
David Salariya was born in Dundee, Scotland. He has illustrated a wide range of books and has created and designed many new series for publishers both in the U.K. and overseas. In 1989, he established The Salariya Book Company. He lives in Brighton with his wife, illustrator Shirley Willis, and their son Jonathan.

Editor:
Karen Barker Smith

Created, designed, and produced by
The Salariya Book Company Ltd
Book House, 25 Marlborough Place
Brighton BN1 1UB

Please visit The Salariya Book Company at:
www.salariya.com

ISBN 0-531-12312-X (Lib. Bdg.)
ISBN 0-531-16651-1 (Pbk.)

Published in the United States by Franklin Watts
A Division of Scholastic Inc.
90 Sherman Turnpike, Danbury, CT 06816

A CIP catalog record for this title is available from the Library of Congress.

Printed and bound in China.

Printed on paper from sustainable forests.

You Wouldn't Want to Be in a Medieval Dungeon!

Criminals, traitors, and outlaws better watch out!

Prisoners You'd Rather Not Meet

Written by
Fiona Macdonald

Illustrated by
David Antram

Created and designed by
David Salariya

W
FRANKLIN WATTS
A Division of Scholastic Inc.

NEW YORK • TORONTO • LONDON • AUCKLAND • SYDNEY
MEXICO CITY • NEW DELHI • HONG KONG
DANBURY, CONNECTICUT

Contents

Introduction 5

A Career Change 6

Who Will You Work For? 8

Types of Prisons 10

Castle Life 12

Criminals, Traitors, and Outlaws 14

Bad Company 16

Innocent Victims 18

Dealing With Prisoners 20

Rats, Lice, and Fleas 22

The Soft Option 24

No Escape! 26

Freedom or Death 28

Glossary 30

Index 32

Introduction

It is the end of the 15th century in medieval England. You are a tough, battle-scarred soldier who has just returned home after fighting wars in far-away countries. You are happy to have survived even though your shoulder has been badly wounded and your arm is broken.

You won't be much use as a fighter from now on, but your injuries are healing and you start to feel better. You are also feeling poor! You have spent all of your soldier's wages and have nothing to live on. You need to find a job so you decide to go to the nearest castle to see what jobs are available there. You're in luck! The castle needs someone to help run its prison. The captain of the guard asks if you would like the job. Think carefully! Do you really want to work in a medieval jail?

A Career Change

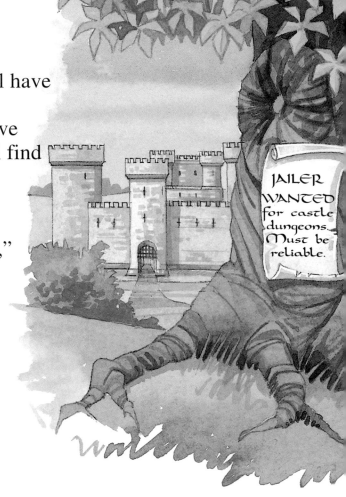

If you become a castle jailer you will have to work hard and learn quickly. The job is not well paid, but you have power over your prisoners. You will find many ways of making extra money by demanding bribes and charging fees. There is a good chance of promotion. Experienced prison wardens and "turnkeys," or security guards, are in demand — most castles, cities, and towns have at least one jail. There are plenty of other people who would like the job, too.

JAILER WANTED for castle dungeons. Must be reliable.

Applicants for the Job:

AN OLD SERVANT. He knows the castle well and has worked here since he was a boy.

A CRUSADER. Back home after fighting wars in the Middle East, he needs a new job.

A PRIEST. Clever and cunning, he is on the lookout for people who break church laws.

A MONK. He is in charge of the punishment cell at the local monastery.

A NIGHT WATCHMAN. He guards the castle gates and is looking for a promotion.

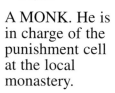

I'd steer clear of that place if I were you. Some of those prisoners are a nasty lot!

Handy Hint
Women need not apply! Only men can be jailers in the Middle Ages.

AN IRONWORKER. He has made all the metal bars that stop prisoners from escaping.

A POLICE OFFICER. He works for the sheriff and arrests people who break the law.

A LOCAL TOWNSMAN. He hopes to make money by working at the jail.

A TRUSTED OFFICIAL. Elegant and polite, he would be good at dealing with captive nobles and royalty.

A THUG. He will frighten the prisoners but they will probably outwit him.

Who Will You Work For?

Like all medieval jailers, you will not have special training. If you get the job it will be because the person who owns the prison thinks you can be trusted. Your employer will most likely be the king. It is his duty to maintain law and order and to protect his kingdom from traitors, rebels, and foreign enemies. Most prisons, county jails, and dungeons in all the royal castles in London belong to him. Many other powerful people have their own private prisons, too.

Possible Employers

LORDS AND LADIES rule the land around their castles and have their own private prisons. They can punish minor crimes, such as trespassing, slander, and non-payment of rent.

Lady *Lord* *Commander*

ARMY COMMANDERS imprison enemy captives and demand a ransom to set them free.

TOWN COUNSELORS are in charge of town prisons and are eager to punish merchants' crimes, such as fraud and theft.

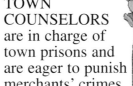

Counselor

Bishop

BISHOPS can imprison people who break the church's religious laws. The bishops often get involved in quarrels over church land and property.

ABBOTS AND ABBESSES are in charge of religious communities. If monks and nuns break the rules, they are locked in punishment cells.

Religious Investigator

Abbot

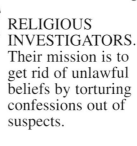

RELIGIOUS INVESTIGATORS. Their mission is to get rid of unlawful beliefs by torturing confessions out of suspects.

SHERIFFS act as the king's deputy in each county. Criminals are held in a royal prison until the king's judges hold a trial.

Sheriff

8

IN MEDIEVAL ENGLAND the king's word is law! The most important royal court is called the "King's Bench." It gets its name from the seat used by top royal judges, who try suspects accused of serious crimes. Sometimes the king himself sits in the court.

Royal judges

Types of Prisons

Oubliette

Once you start work, you will soon discover that prisons are not all the same. In castles, prison cells are often built above the main gates in the outer walls. This way, dangerous prisoners do not get too close to the castle keep, or the central tower of the castle. Other castle prisons are hidden deep below ground or in high towers. Sometimes cells are just metal cages hung outside the castle. King Edward I of England kept the wife of a Scottish noble in a cage like this for over a year! City prisons are often built in drafty vaults below the chambers where counselors meet. Empty buildings are sometimes turned into prisons.

AN OUBLIETTE (left) is a narrow, tube-shaped prison, without windows. The only way in is through a trapdoor at the top. Prisoners are lowered down on a rope and left to rot! Sometimes water seeps in from the bottom and they drown.

YOU MIGHT have to shut prisoners in a "little ease" — a tiny room hollowed out of castle walls (right). Some of these cramped chambers are so small that prisoners cannot lie down, sit comfortably, or even turn around.

Bottle dungeon

Handy Hint

Once you have gained experience, give advice to builders and architects. They might pay you for tips on how to make a prison really secure.

Bottle dungeons (left) are deep underground prisons. Tall stone towers (right) keep prisoners high in the air. Both are designed to prevent escapes and hide prisoners away from friends who might help them.

What have I done to deserve this?

SOME CASTLES have private rooms where rich or noble prisoners are locked up in nice surroundings. They may even be allowed to stroll in the castle's gardens (above).

Little ease

11

Castle Life

Life in a medieval castle is extremely busy. It is like a whole village community inside strong stone walls. There is never a quiet moment, from sunrise to after dark. There are soldiers shouting, blacksmiths hammering, horses whinnying, pigs grunting, babies crying, women chattering, workmen grumbling, messengers complaining and, above it all, the lord of the castle barking out commands. Heavy farm carts, full of vital supplies, rumble over the stone courtyard. Laborers grunt and sweat as they unload sacks of grain. It's no wonder you can't sleep in your off-duty hours!

Criminals, Traitors, and Outlaws

As a jailer, you'll have to deal with people accused of many different crimes. There are highway robbers, counterfeiters, traitors, and other "enemies of the state." All will have been arrested on suspicion and put in prison to wait for months or years for judges to arrive. Take care! Many prisoners will be angry and violent and some of them are dangerous. All will be frightened that one day soon, they might die. Death is the punishment for serious crimes such as murder, treason, forgery, or robbery with violence.

Dead Scared

All these prisoners (right) face the death penalty if they are found guilty. People who commit less serious crimes are fined, flogged, or left to rot in prison for a while.

Pirate *Murderer* *Burglar*

Traitor or rebel   Plotter   Outlaw   Counterfeiter   Corrupt official

Bad Company

You will probably believe that most of your prisoners are bad even though many of them have not committed a crime. Some are in prison because they have powerful enemies. People are also imprisoned because they are thought to be witches or have strange beliefs. Some prisoners will be there because of bad luck. Other prisoners are guilty but hardship and poverty might have forced them into stealing or breaking the law. However, like most medieval people, you think that people should accept their fate and have no excuse to break the law.

STEALING SHEEP. A nice fat sheep makes a tempting target for hungry thieves. It can feed a poor family for at least a week.

STOP, THIEF!

LIFE IS HORRIBLE for ordinary people in the Middle Ages. Most are poor and many are not free to leave their lord's lands. They are often cold, tired, and hungry. It is not surprising that some become criminals.

THE CATHOLIC CHURCH is powerful throughout Europe. Church leaders believe that only they know the truth about God. Anyone with different beliefs is guilty of heresy, which is a deadly sin.

Handy Hint

See what advice you can get from "witches" in your prison. Such people often know about healing herbs, poisons, and "magic spells."

HOME LIFE can be stressful. Many people have arranged marriages. Whatever their feelings, husbands and wives have to stay together or starve. There is no state welfare system so poverty drives people to commit crime.

SOLDIERS CAPTURED IN BATTLE face a gloomy future. They will be kept in prison until their families pay a ransom to set them free. If they cannot afford to do this, then the soldiers may be killed.

Only 126 miles to go.

Innocent Victims

It is hard to dislike all your prisoners – some are innocent victims with heartbreaking stories. Often these people have found themselves behind bars because somebody powerful wants them out of the way. Maybe they have angered the royal family or know embarrassing secrets. Perhaps they have rival claims to inherit a rich estate or even the throne! Many such prisoners are women and children. The young English princes (right), Edward, age 12, and Richard, age 9, were locked in the Tower of London by their uncle, King Richard III, in 1483. He had them murdered so they could not grow up and take over the throne.

SHIPWRECKED SAILORS are arrested and locked up until they can prove who they are.

FRIENDS who have quarreled with someone powerful may be carried off to jail.

WOMEN WHO REJECT royal offers of love or marriage might be put in prison until they change their minds.

FOREIGN AMBASSADORS are sent to prison when wars begin. They were friends to the state before war but have since become enemies.

ROYAL WIVES who fail to give birth to a son might be jailed because they are useless!

PEOPLE WITH MENTAL ILLNESSES are locked up to keep them safe, but others cruelly come to laugh at them.

Dealing With Prisoners

Medieval prisons are terrible places. Most prisoners will beg you to set them free or at least move them out of the damp, dark, crowded cells. You must be hardhearted. If you let anyone escape, you'll lose your job, be beaten, or even executed!

I'll give you anything you want if I get out of here, just for a piece of that pie!

CONDITIONS INSIDE jails are disgusting. Most jailers do not care! If prisoners cannot arrange for someone to bring them food, candles, and bedding, they will suffer terribly.

Cells are slimy...

damp...

dark...

and crowded!

Prisoners will plead for food, water, and other basic comforts, such as straw to sleep on or the chance to warm themselves by a fire in winter. Nothing — no food, water, or bedding — is supplied by the owner of the jail. Prisoners' friends and families must provide these supplies. You can offer to get supplies, if the prisoners pay you!

Handy Hint

Don't keep a dog or a cat – they'll chase the rats and mice away! You want your prison to be as nasty as possible!

YOU CAN MAKE extra money by demanding a fee from the friends, business colleagues, and lawyers who visit prisoners (left).

YOU MIGHT LET starving prisoners beg for food through the bars of their cells (right). With luck, passers-by will take pity on them.

No beds

No toilets

Rats, Lice, and Fleas

You need a strong stomach and a strong mind to cope with prison conditions. Most cells are infested with insects, and most prisoners are covered with lice or fleas. Rats, lizards, beetles, and cockroaches scurry across the damp, dirty floors. As well as scaring sensitive prisoners, these creatures can carry serious diseases. The worst are typhus fever and plague, also known as the Black Death! Many prisoners die from disease before they ever go to trial. Prisons are also very smelly. Inside, they reek of stale blood, sweat, and sewage. Outside most prison walls, you can't escape the smell of stagnant moats, blocked drains, toilets, and stables.

RAIN, SNOW, and cold, damp air blows through the prison bars and chills everyone locked up inside. Many prisoners die from hypothermia, or extremely low body temperature.

FLEAS carry plague germs in their saliva. Lice carry the germs that cause typhus fever. If the bugs bite you, you will catch these diseases.

RATS also carry plague, a terrible illness. Victims get huge boils on their groins and armpits, bleed from the mouth (and elsewhere), run a high temperature, become delirious, and die.

DIRTY, SMELLY WATER carries germs and tiny microorganisms that cause vomiting and diarrhea. Prisoners have to risk drinking it – or die of thirst.

The Soft Option

Sometimes it's a good idea to treat prisoners kindly, especially those who might be in a position to help you if they're set free. Even the most powerful men and women will be grateful if you make their stay in prison as comfortable as possible. Let them bring their own books, furniture, musical instruments, servants, and children. Let them continue to have a hobby or work. Top tailors imprisoned in London bring their sewing kits with them so that they can still make clothes for customers. This way they earn money to pay for luxuries while they are behind bars.

EVEN THE MOST COMFORTABLE PRISONS can be dangerous places. Poison or "accidents" are the most usual methods of quietly getting rid of important prisoners.

Is there anything I can do for you, m'lady?

EXERCISE stops prisoners growing restless and dangerous. The guards at Fleet prison in London, let rich prisoners play skittles all day long. Skittles is a game that is similar to bowling.

WIVES AND MOTHERS often ask to bring food in for their families. Let them do this, but search the meals for hidden weapons or tools.

FRIARS need your permission to preach and say prayers in prison. Welcome them! Their holy words might help your sinful soul.

24

What a creep!

Handy Hint

There will be some visitors your prisoners don't want to see, such as enemies who could taunt or bully them. Offer to keep them out – for a fee!

LOOK FORWARD to a better job! You may get this as a reward from powerful people you have helped in jail.

YOU CAN EXPECT gifts and bribes in return for treating prisoners kindly, but don't be too greedy!

BE POLITE to important people, even if they are prisoners. They might be powerful again one day.

No Escape!

There are plenty of ways to ensure your prisoners are secure. To begin with, you'll rely on heavy wooden doors with strong locks and bolts and iron bars across all the windows. You will probably choose to keep the most dangerous or high risk prisoners fastened to cell walls, using handcuffs and leg-fetters that are attached to heavy iron chains. If you are cruel you can arrange for these to be fixed so prisoners can't move or touch the floor.

To force prisoners to confess to crimes jailers use torture. The most common tortures are: the red-hot iron, which burns; the rack, which stretches prisoners and destroys their joints; the boot, which crushes prisoners' legs; and thumbscrews, which squeeze fingers until the fingernails fall off.

Leg-fetters

> This might sting just a little bit...

Pillory

Stocks

Ducking stool

Other Punishments

THIEVES can be locked in a pillory (above left) where their heads and hands are trapped while the public throws garbage at them. Or you could shut them in the stocks (above right) so that everyone they've cheated can pelt them with mud and rotten food.

IF A WOMAN is known to be a gossip, tie her to a ducking stool (left) and dip her in the river. That will teach her to hold her tongue!

27

Freedom or Death

Very few prisoners manage to escape from jail or can pay the ransom money to be set free. Those with powerful friends can expect to be released if a new king comes to the throne or when new politicians win power. Most prisoners find that death is the only way out of jail. They die in prison from cold, hunger, torture, or disease – or they are executed. Noble men and women are beheaded, which is quick and almost painless. Ordinary criminals are condemned to be hanged – a slow, very painful way to die.

Can't we talk about this...?

Not guilty

SOME PRISONERS' get out of jail more peacefully. They might be found not guilty and set free. They might be forgiven for their crimes and receive a royal pardon. They might escape in disguise, or they might die and be free from suffering at last.

Handy Hint

Retire as soon as you can! As a jailer, you'll have made many enemies. Some people will want revenge – you don't want to end up in jail yourself!

Death

Escape in disguise

A pardon

SAVED BY A SONG! King Richard the Lionheart of England (ruled 1189-1199) was captured by enemies while returning from a war. No one knew where he was being held. Legend says that his minstrel traveled Europe singing Richard's favorite song while looking for him. When the king sang back, the minstrel knew he had found him!

Glossary

Abbess The leader of a religious community of nuns.

Abbot The leader of a religious community of monks.

Ambassador A senior government official sent to represent his or her king and country overseas.

Bottle dungeon A deep underground prison, shaped like an old-fashioned bottle. Prisoners entered through a narrow "bottle neck" and were kept captive in the globe-shaped chamber below.

Bribe A payment made in return for a special favor.

Counterfeiter A person that makes fake money.

Crusader A soldier who fought in wars in the Middle East between Christian and Muslim armies.

Fetters Curved iron bars that could be locked around prisoners' legs.

Flogged Severely beaten.

Fraud Cheating.

Friar A priest who lived close to poor and needy people in medieval communities.

Heresy Unlawful religious beliefs. In the Middle Ages that included any beliefs that were different to those of the people in power.

Jail Another word for prison.

Keep The strong central tower of a castle.

Medieval Belonging to the Middle Ages (the years from around A.D. 1000 to A.D. 1500).

Middle Ages (see **Medieval** above).

Minstrel A medieval traveling musician who played an instrument and performed songs and poetry.

Outlaw A criminal who lives outside the normal rules of law.

Pardon To excuse or forgive someone for a wrongdoing and release them from punishment.

Plague A deadly and infectious disease which was very widespread in the Middle Ages.

Ransom A demand for money in order to let prisoners go free.

Slander Telling lies about someone.

Stocks A low wooden frame that has holes in it for a criminal's feet. Offenders were locked in the stocks as a punishment.

Tenant A person who rents land and property from the person who owns it.

Traitor A person who betrays their country. In the Middle Ages, people who betrayed their local lord or their employer might be accused of being traitors. A wife who betrayed her husband could also be considered a traitor.

Trespass To enter someone's private property without permission.

Vaults Cellars or underground rooms.

Index

A
abbots and abbesses 8

B
bishops 8
bottle dungeons 11
bribes 6, 9, 21, 24, 25

C
captive enemies 8, 17, 18
castles 5, 6, 8, 10, 11, 12, 13
church laws 8, 16
constables 7
criminals 9, 14, 15, 16, 17, 28
Crusader 6

D
death penalty 14, 15, 20, 28, 29
dirt and disease 20, 21, 22, 23,
   28
dungeon (*see* prison)

E
escape 11, 20, 26, 28, 29

F
fines 14
flogging 14
food and water 20, 21, 23, 24

G
guards 5, 6, 13

H
heresy 8, 16

I
innocent victims 18, 19
ironworkers 7

J
jail (*see* prison)
judges 8, 9

K
kings 8, 9, 18, 28, 29

L
law and order 8, 9, 14, 15
little ease 10, 11
living conditions 16, 17
locks and chains 26, 27

M
mental illness 18, 19
monks 6, 8

N
nobles 7, 8, 10, 11, 12, 18, 24,
   25, 28

O
oubliette 10
outlaws 14, 15

P
pardon 29
pillory 27
poison 24
priests 6, 18, 24
prisoners 6, 7, 14, 15, 16, 17, 18,
   19, 20, 21, 22, 23, 24, 25, 26,
   27, 28, 29
prisons 5, 6, 8, 10, 11, 14, 20,
   21, 22, 23, 24, 25, 26, 28
   conditions 20, 21, 22. 23, 24,
      25, 26
   design 10, 11, 26, 27
promotion 6, 25

R
ransom 28
rats 21, 22, 23
retirement 29

S
sheriffs 8
smells 22, 23
soldiers 5, 12, 17, 19
stocks 27

T
torture 25, 26, 28
towers 10, 11
town counselors 8
training 8
traitors 8, 14, 15

V
visitors 19, 25

W
witches 16, 17
women 6, 10, 11, 12, 15, 17, 18,
   19, 24, 27, 28